On Beacon Street

On Beacon Street

A Collection of Poetry

Sarah Brashear

Cawing
Crow
Press

To Marla,

A great
tennis player
and friend.
I love your
positive
altitude!

♡ Sarah
Brashear

© 2015 by Sarah Brashear

For permission requests, email the publisher, at: inquiry@cawingcrowpress.com

Published by:

Cawing Crow Press LLC

Dunlo, PA

ISBN: 978-1-68264-003-6

Library of Congress Control Number: 2015955453

Visit us on the web at: www.cawingcrowpress.com

Acknowledgements

The author acknowledges the following magazines in which the following poems, or previous versions of these poems first appeared:

Brickplight: "Arrow Landing", Burningword Press: "Beacon Street Lake", Duende: "Meth", Driftwood Press: "*Let's pretend the mountains are our husbands*", Etched Press: "This Frayed Universe Chapbook", Gravel: "On The Death of Salem", Misfit Magazine "Beacon Street Annual Cocktail Party", Nerve Cowboy "My Mother's Surgery", Off The Coast "Mad Boy Stirs", The Red Clay Review: "Holy Communion", The Riding Light Review: "Danse Macabre", "Children don't play Marco Polo around here, they play Charlie Pyle", Rufous City Review: "Autism", Sediments: "Here, In The Realm of Everything

I dedicate this book of poetry to my parents, Daniel and Linda Grodzinski for supporting me and letting me follow my creative path of education and reach my dreams of being a poet. I also dedicate this book to my Nana, Nancy Hickey and my Grandma, Julia Albert, who have consistently encouraged me to keep writing and exploring my creativity. They never let me give up on my dream of publishing a book. Lastly, I dedicate this book to my other half, my husband, Adam.

Introduction

On Beacon Street explores a narrator living on Beacon Street and her relationship with family, friends, and members of the community. The poems explore the landscape and the people living in this fictional town, as well as the narrator's intimate relationship and connection with people and nature. She also recalls stories from her childhood, telling of these quirky, everyday people that reside on Beacon Street. These narratives mirror the reputation of any small town community in the United States. I hope people will relate to the characters and stories explored in this book. My poetry is image heavy and I like to write about the unusual; the cryptic people we encounter in everyday life. I have always been a vivid dreamer. I like the haunted moments in dreams that stay with you. These moments are what I like to write about. I am also interested in the unusual, and I am drawn to eccentric people. This darkness I am trying to replicate in my writing is fleeting. It comes and goes as quickly as the breath leaves a mouth after a scream. The desire to recreate these moments on the page is where my writing stems from.

Table of Contents

The Poems

On Beacon Street, Part I

The children are hawks.
They point, stare, throw bits of trash.
Tim's small with freckles, Al's all arms and eyes.
They run to Old Man Tucker's house and pelt rocks.

Old Man Tucker sits in his canyon, face spinning.
His lip is severed, but he still shouts.
I'm not afraid of his sadness;
I just don't know what to do with it.

The kids who pass his trailer grabble
run away falling on the lawn in laughter.
I always feel bad and go back later,
listen to his stories and water his plants.

He has a bull's eye tattoo above his collar bone,
tells me he got it during the war.
I ask about the Germans, he tells me
the explosions bit his ear.

It makes sense.
When I see him three days later,
and his neighbor's car alarm goes off—
He flinches.

I. The People

Arrow Landing

As a child, I climbed down to Arrow Landing and jumped
in the crick on days when summer baked our minds.

Duke was always there. I watched him catch grasshoppers
and dare the younger kids to eat them.

Their eyes grew wide and they ran home crying,
tongues hanging out of their mouths in trepidation.

The heat sucked our shirts to our bodies, pit stains
formed like crop circles on our sleeves.

Sometimes Duke brought bottles of Pabst
and we let the cool froth dribble down our tongues.

When a new kid came to town, we hazed him,
forced him to swing from the rope into

"The Lagoon" where torrents of water thrashed below
and rumor had it several kids had drowned.

One time there was an old Rattler tucked under the mud,
we didn't hear him until he was within inches of our ribs.

I held my breath until I watched him slither by,
his slanted eyes staring. Duke crept behind me

his braces shining in the sunlight, his breath on my neck
as he whispered in my ear, "Dare you to touch the snake."

Beacon Baptist Church

Everything Aunt Alda holds in the Bible
of her brain shakes static.

She speaks to the boilers
half expecting them to reply.
Dark marks on the paneling
are liver spots; they grow in rings.

She forgets to turn off the burner
after lighting her cigarette.
Can no longer remember which state
the Yankees play for,
or the name of the church
where she was married,

but she remembers God.
Hears Him hang above her.
He is a bat. She listens
to Gloria Patri, tries to sing along,
sits on her stairs, rubs cream
across her chest instead
of her face, and turns off the lamp
instead of the tap.

The Salt Man

When it snows on Beacon Street,
the salt crystals crunch
underneath soggy car tires.
Old Joe takes his shovel and barrow
and pours the pieces over
the sidewalks, ensuring our safety.

He doesn't say much,
just nods and thinks of his son,
who died in an automobile accident
during an ice storm.
The winded flavor of grief
still sticks to the back of his throat.

His hands are wrought iron,
scratched by the cold,
his murky face made of shale, body drenched
in the cool sweat of Wild Turkey Bourbon.
Voice taut, ripped from the wire,
he's been up since dawn covering the streets
with his sadness.

There ain't no blues but the ones behind you
he hears on the radio.

He turns his head, spits tobacco into a tin can,
and looks out at the navel of night sky.
The stars fold into
tiny beams of cavernous light.

On the anniversary of his son's death
it's all he can do, as he passes us on
the sidewalk,
to close his eyes
pick up his shovel
and cover our frozen tracks.

Miss Penny

Every day he drives nine miles
to the Moxy Wellness Center
and takes his paraplegic sister swimming.

Her spine is a fishhook.
She bucks and frolics in the water.
The chlorine is a stimulant to the nerves
in her body that are damaged.

The lack of oxygen when
she holds her breath
reminds her that he is the lifeline
that keeps her together.

Penny's hair slaps against the water
like a mop, she squirms along the
surface, craving his hand
to pick her back out of the pool,
so she can take a breath—

but there's a stirring deep inside her,
a glimmer of hope that perhaps,
he'll be distracted,
the lifeguard will be asleep,
and her brother will forget
to let her come up for air.

Mr. Shutler

He's like Boo Radley—
all quiet eyes and thin mouthed,
placing clips of paper in a tree.

He lives by the river
goes fishing twice a day;
heard he catches them with a spear.

He thinks he's an Indian,
although we're not sure which tribe.
I watch him scream a war cry,

and shiver as paint drips down his face
into a perfect red mask.
He throws stones at us from the hilltop.

They land as lumps in the water,
mud splashes around the surface.
We all have a story about him.

I remember bird watching
in middle school, out by
the state park

I was looking for a red-tailed hawk
when I found my gaze
drifting toward his pent-in house.

I looked through the window,
saw him holding his own pair
of binoculars, met his eyes

watching me from inside,
blinds drawn,
pants down to his ankles.

To My Aging Father

Because your arms were sagging
as you lifted the heavy bricks
off the furnace, off your chest
and let the crumbles of concrete rain
down at your feet.
Because the air was heavy, like meringue
and your strength was waning
three years after the day you found her,
muttering recipes, her cookbook
open to eggplant parmigiana,
her eyes wobbling like a bowling ball
along a waxy lane.
You used that metaphor often,
the ball knocking down the pins,
one by one.
Your life slipping back
into the gutter.

Grandpa's Den

The wallpaper behind him is spackled.
The flames of the fire remind
him of the ventilator beside her bed
which shot up and down.

When she left him
her mouth was soft, half open
his own ribs cracked at her breaking.
Like a colander, his life sifted
through the holes left in his heart.

Now there is snow in the distance,
the calendar on the wall anchors endless days of white.
He thinks of how her hands held the wine glass.
How she tasted like its tannins.
He thinks it strange
he should sip without her.
This, the life they have fermented.

Visiting Grandpa at His Home on a Tuesday Morning

On his rocker, my grandpa is relentless.
He breaks the hours with chatter,
talks about his childhood,
when his younger brother fell off the slide
at the playground and needed stitches.

He scratches his chin—unshaven and dried with spittle,
and recalls how he could have stopped the accident.
He shows me how he clung
to the monkey bars in awe,
watched his baby brother's face splinter.

He maneuvered his weight back and forth
on those rust-caked bars, climbing eighteen rungs.
He didn't let go, chose not to
save his brother's chin from hitting the ground.

Back in the living room, Grandpa spreads his fingers,
shows me the hint of dry ash still on his palms,
picks up my hand
and has me feel the callused skin
where the blood formed years ago.
His muscles ached, his forehead perspired
but he tells me, on those bars, he felt safe.

The Mechanic's Daughter

She learned more about cars than she knew about men
in the dusty old mechanic shop her Pop owned.

She found out how to breathe exhaust fumes,
and run her fingers along ratty old tires,
how to tie ropes onto parts and fix *corroborators*.

She learned sometimes you had to run sand through the engine
and patiently wait for it to stutter and start
long after you turned the key in the ignition.

She rode her first car at the age of nine,
four years before she kissed a boy,
eight years before she slept with one.

She's still unsure where to place her hands
while he's inside her, but the fabric cover
on the steering wheel always feels familiar.

She tries to find similarities,
riding her Ford Mustang, the chrome wheels
flashing silver as she sinks
into the plush leather seats.
As she cruises down Interstate 95
at almost ninety miles an hour,
she thinks, no ride
will ever feel this smooth.

Mad Boy Stirs

The morning they take Dan
he's eating a flower.
The pollen leaves yellow stains
around his lips.
Smiling, he grabs fistfuls of grass
to keep himself balanced.

He claws with wild eyes,
refuses the Earth's medicines
of orange lava drops and pesticides.
Not a whole person but
a quarantined half.
The bell rings for supper, he comes.
The light flickers in the hall. The small peel
stretches over him, a silkworm.
He slips across the soft feather of floor
that holds him upright.

The red hot strips of winter burn his feet.
He's walking on ice,
too dark to be full of day.
Electric blue pills, belly up
clink in his hands, like ice crystals.

He's a Golden Chain Tree,
his branches
grow out of me, arms flake, limbs flail.
To be the sweat that sticks to him,
bark that spills from him,
black cherry smoke that spins in circles
as his eyes shut to the world.

Every morning he jumps over torches
and midday he's caught by candlelight.
He burns, he burns, he burns.

Autism

Sunday, at the Beacon Street Market
I watch as Daniel is pushed in his wagon,
limp feet hang off the side--two empty spigots.

He gazes in wonder at the people,
collects stamps that fall on the ground,
licks the backs of them, and sticks them to his stomach.
They hide under the loose wind of his shirt.

Dan doesn't speak, just gazes at the close-up faces
of people selling records and scarves,
photographs, and old rotary phones.

He was born into a land that calls him
by his father's name, cauliflower cheeks tuck behind
great stamen lashes that magnify his face.
His eyes tilt away from the noise.

When handed a balloon,
he brings it to his mouth,
bites the red rubber until it pops, shrivels, and
dangles like licorice off his tongue.

The Minister's Son

He could control his congregation,
but never his child.
He ran amuck in the streets.

A liquid boy with the best intentions
coral beams, drops for eyes,
and a smile that ran across his face like a saw.

His crimes were small at first:
a missing coin, stolen lawn ornaments.
As the calendar year flipped through

we all became a little suspicious.
New in town, his father was a riot,
a hearty laugh and plenty of meat on his bones.

I always noticed the crease that wrinkled
in his forehead and the way his eyebrows
raised when he talked in the sanctuary.

But the boy drew crowds wherever he went, so
nobody was surprised
when school was closed early

that December morning, the snow pale
in our eyes except for bits of blood
that fell from the fallen body,

and the owner of the Glock glaring
at us with that same snide smirk
and a tattered hymnal in his hands.

Reflections

Old Man Tucker fell asleep
with the bear mask on.
I rubbed the mottled brown fur
around the ears.
I watched him breathe, chest
rising and falling,
the rhythm
of a dragonfly.

He comes from a place where God
holds his body, brave in the magma of
the new world. His almond eyes
and shriveled tongue crave for an
existence that carries
beyond his sleeping limbs.

I watched him to make
sure he was really out,
picked off the mask,
walked to the mirror,
and slid it over my head.
I felt my fur, the frayed edges
sticky from his fingers,
which were always
full of something.
I looked at my new
body and smiled.
The ugly animal
grinning back.

Danse Macabre

Growing up on Beacon Street
I thought the mailman was a ghost.
I heard his soft feet nuzzle the ground
his pallor skin fell faint with freckles.
One time, I climbed the apple tree by
the graveyard and looked out and saw him
in the confines of tombstones, lurking,
a shadowed body in a tallboy frame.

I heard rumors he could dance.
That the floor beneath him fell.
When he lifted his legs everyone else
stopped moving.
I spied on him, thought:
if the dead can do anything,
they can dance.

I fell asleep by the cornfield
the swaying rhythm of the stalks
brushing against my collarbone
reminding me of a salsa.
I felt him shake me awake
that evening.
I screamed.
He put his face close to my ear.
I could feel his cold breath buffeting my neck.
"Do you believe in Ghosts?" he smiled, all broken and black teeth.

My Mother's Surgery

I imagined her
in the blue display case.
A microwave plate will spin her around.
When it beeps I'll wait for her heated body to cool.

The doctors will pick at her brain,
cut the wires, the wires, feed her
through tubes until she's able to swallow.
Stuck inside the wormhole.

After her surgery, I step into the room.
I am reminded of nights by Beacon Baptist Cemetery
when I learned what fear was; nights
ghost spirits rolled out of bodies like spools of thread.

Moans launch out of her body,
stir the blinds, send the bugs in the wrong direction.
I watch the IV drip, liquid through a straw.

Her wire-spun hair is static, the sap of
her spit, anything but nectar. Her mouth
opens and closes involuntarily, her pliant
tongue utters, "You're a Grand Old Flag."

Siblings

In seventh grade I gave you the nickname
Chubby Checkers, told your girlfriend,
and you didn't speak to me for a month.
You used to chase me up and down the street
with fire poppers, cracking the backs of my knees
and my shoulder blades.

We survived mostly on *Roseanne*.
Watched old reruns with mom in her
chair, we took turns refilling her wine glass
sometimes sneaking in little sips,
so we had the tolerance to deal
with whatever orders she snapped at us next.

I remember one December, you told me
you were hungry, and all we had left in the house
was stale bread and some juice,
so I walked through the snowstorm
to the 7-11 and used my allowance
to buy us each a hot dog and a fountain soda.
You didn't chase me then,
and I didn't tease you with nicknames.
We just sat in the quiet neon store
watching the snow fall, letting
our mouths fill with sweet cherry syrup.

Old Man Tucker

The war left him as burnt as a piece of steak
smoking on the grill,
grease stained with marks from
where the spatula gun had slapped him.

They took his right arm
but not his dignity.
It's been forty months
without a glass of gin or a cigarette.

He holds prayer meetings
at the local high school,
volunteers at the humane society
twice a week.
Most days, he grows attached
to Sniper, a yellow lab
who is terrified of the other dogs.

Old Man Tucker cares for the mutt as if it were
part of his squad, (unit thirty-four).
He pats him behind the ears,
looks at him with those eyes, as if to say
You have no idea what I've been through.

Sniper runs to the nearest tree,
lifts his leg and starts to urinate.
The wetness circles the cracked earth.
Old Man Tucker reaches for the leash.

Sniper's teeth come at the old man in a snap,
scrape through his skin.
He slips from his half-hold on the branch
as he gradually sinks down into the mud.

Kitchen Crawler

I need fish gills for when the flood starts
he says, skims over the Old Testament.

My brother doesn't understand religion,
but neither do I.

He dances in the kitchen,
wears a chrome sauce pan on his head.

Tears apart the place mats, throws the silverware.
The forks explode off the cabinets.

I thought if I fell asleep with my hands
in prayer, when I awoke

God would still be listening.
(He wasn't). God says gluttony is a sin.

My brother eats sugar and cold meats. A gut
swings loosely—a pendulum.

He's ravenous in the evenings,
falls asleep by the refrigerator.

A half-eaten leg of chicken still in his hand,
gravy slides down his mouth, glues to his chin.

If I try to wake him, he hits me,
hung over on calories and carbohydrates.

He wobbles back to the kitchen,
tells me to sleep. I pretend, but watch

as he drags his body across the floor
opens the door to his safe.

The clear gleam of a bulb shines,
a spotlight reveals yesterday's pot pie.

In the park behind Mr. Shutler's house

When I was nine
I saw two boys from high school in the sandbox.
I thought I saw them slip a plastic bag,
from their tongues,
thought maybe it was drugs.

These were my brother's friends,
guys who picked on me and my band friends,
guys who played football, who didn't have time
to date the cheerleaders because they
already had college girlfriends.

So when I saw them out my window
while I was doing homework,
I thought maybe I could join them—
have my own taste at a silver coin.

As I approached their dark figures
in the sandbox, ready for the relief,
I heard one of them moan,
saw the rise and the fall of his body
and noticed the belt's buckle
poking through the sand.

I crept backward, slowly,
circling my dry tongue around my mouth
trying to swallow.
I ran up to my room
and finished my spelling homework.

The Dancer

The way she danced—like bells swaying
atop a tower,
on a twisted lilt of night sky,
could hunger any man.

Her sozzled sighs
rhymed with the cadence of
the evening, and she spent
most of her mornings,

with a hangover, in the attic,
tearing through photographs
that reminded her of when
she was a kid, lively and dynamic,
stucco red cheeks glowing
in the full lush of summer.

She used to stare at these pictures,
in the homespun air of Beacon Street
her radiant visions of
going to Julliard
diminishing, as the rain
rattled against the roof
in a stony silence.

The bottlenecked traffic
slowly made its way to work.
She found her way to the kitchen
to cook breakfast,
iron her tights
watch the morning news.

Chemistry

The first time she saw his face—
unshaven and one chipped tooth,
she knew she was in it for the long haul.

They were always at war,
slaying each other with stares,
grinding and grabbing
happy only when the heat from the flame was gone.

In the kitchen she wasn't afraid
to show her contempt, burning the pans, rattling utensils,
and if she was angry enough, undercooking
the flank steaks so they were pink
as a newborn's lips.

She was a philanderess at heart,
always walking into the wrong aisle,
interrupting a love that wasn't hers to take.

She recalls the day in the dairy section
of Walgreens with perfect cleavage,
and skin the color of navel oranges
when she brushed the science teacher's hand
as she reached for a carton of eggs.

That feeling—the tingle in her body,
like an ornament glowing on a tree,
left her satisfied.

On the death of Salem

I take the train to get to the city.
It passes the monuments, the buildings, the buzz and the blur.
The leaves on the trees look like soggy crowns
as they slump on the shoulders of worn branches.
I grip the handles of my reusable grocery bag the whole way,
afraid of what will happen when I get out and
walk inside the vet's office,
and leave this canine frame on the table.
It was his idea to put the dog in this shopping bag.

The smell wafts through the zippered lining,
the stares gather from the man with the loud ear buds
who bobs his head up and down
and the woman with the bright lipstick
who files her nails, the red crumbs of polish
falling in debris on the steps.
In a way, I almost enjoy the attention,
the scrunched noses, the looks of astonishment
when I tell them I'm taking my dead dog
to the veterinarian because I don't have
the room to bury him in my yard.

In a way, I think it's apropos
that the mother in front of me holds her son's ears
as he turns his head away and cries;
that the psychiatrist who leaves her office
an hour early to have an affair with another man
has to talk even louder than usual
into her cell phone to block out my story.
I think, in a settling, mortifying way
old Salem deserves this.

II.   The Life

On Beacon Street, Part II

The fog that surrounds us is suffocating.
A stroller is being pushed,
joggers sprint across the sidewalks.
A man with a guitar case walks
toward a music shop,
while a lady in scrubs
smokes a cigarette outside of the hospital.
The police officer cocks his head,
with a grin, writes a ticket.
A realtor takes newlyweds
through a house with a manicured lawn.
Above, a lamppost flickers, the bulb
blinks, slowly, leaks out.
They walk down the stairs,
close the door behind them.
This is our chamber of horrors.

Gargoyle

I still contain this fear.
Every night I try to sleep
the sun stains the night sky
into a bloody battlefield.

The stone face of a creature hangs
above the fireplace in the living room,
mouth open like a cannon.
I look at the scowl on the rotten face,
imagine metal balls that spiral,
become a stretched signature in the sky.

I turn on all the lights in the room,
squall, and hide my head under covers.
Midnight scrapes across my body
as I shake off the hurt of the day.

This broken timpani of my heart
is the music I play with my eyes closed.
I'm frantic, unaware of the swaying world.

Later that evening, my father saunters
home from Beacon Street Tavern.
Tired, he crawls, collapses in his clothes,
falls asleep on the couch.

Hours erase. I awake to a scalding earth.
I see his shape shift toward the fireplace
He is holding a hammer.
His shadow spreads across the wall.
I hold my breath and watch
as he lifts the tool over the statue.

Learned Language

In that picture from Mr. Wilder's fourth grade Spanish class our smiles were checkmarks on our faces. You could always roll your r's better than me but I taught you how to speak without sounding American. When we heard lightning, we screamed *relámpago!* That was before they whisked you off to war, and I took my bike home, grabbed my notebooks and wrote your name in the margins.

I was the counter child, sitting next to sinks, below cabinets, helping mom peel carrots and potatoes, but always staring out the window watching the boys play football and wanting so badly to knock one of them to the ground. I remember the year I heard explosions when it wasn't the Fourth of July. Only it wasn't fireworks, and mom threw up into that sink after watching the news, told me to stop talking about you, said you weren't coming back. I ran to my basement, sat beneath the stairwell whispered *relámpago.*

Scabs

In first grade Mom
bought me shoes that didn't fit my feet.
I earned blistered toes for a month and a half
which would bleed, scab over, then rip open again.
It reminded me of the cicada shells I found
lying around the old Sycamore Tree in August.

The first time I picked up a shell—monster-like and ugly,
I screamed and ran for the kitchen.
Mama was baking banana bread, moist heat lofted
toward ceiling fans, drowning me in a vapid aroma
of intoxicating stupor.

I looked at her, with my squinty
eyes and floppy shoes and the cicada balancing
on the tip of my fingers, and I cried.
She walked over, shoved a piece of banana bread
between my lips, told me:
Stop the nonsense, It's only its shell.

I chewed on the bread,
a lump of soggy wafer in my mouth,
and walked back outside pondering this new thought.
I took the shell back to the tree, kicked off my shoes
and ran around the lawn, jumping through weeds.
With bloody toes I abandoned my scabs,
left behind my shell.

Holy Communion

We're closing in on God
you tell me, bite my lip
pull down my skirt,
skin wet as the day
I was born.

I have two loves this summer,
you and a bottle of Jack.

Flowers bud in your breath,
turn your cheeks a shade
of pink I've only ever seen in carnations.

I lie in the latitude of your language.
You keep me until night clogs our vision
the sun's gold brought to my fingertips.

The moon glitters around our eyes
we drop into laps and legs.
Light sends your body glistening
a tingle of seltzer.

I never looked as elegant as I do now,
Eucharist foaming in my throat.

Ashes

When I think of the rain, I think of you
streaming down my body,
a cool rush of betrayal,
mud in my mouth.

Your eyes are the cruel surface of the earth
my hair an un-kept kingdom of holiness.
I've been feeling this way for days, perforated,
alarmed if your hands touched my skin
my secrets would shine through.

That was the day the Ripley's old barn
finally went down in flames.
The day we saw Mr. Ripley on his knees
grabbing fistfuls of grass
and blaspheming the sky.

I felt the slow crawl of heat from the flames
and the sharp exhale of my breath tumbling down
with its siding.

We gathered to watch the disaster,
glad to share in another's suffering
content it wasn't our own.

I heard the thunder before I felt the rain.
It was only then I realized I'd been clenching my fists.
In the glimpse of tragedy I finally relaxed
feeling cleansed, I thought—

If this building, old and decrepit as it was
could finally, after all these years, let go,
eventually I could, too.

Lying In a Tub at Midnight
(After James Wright's Lying in A Hammock...)

We bring the souls down the hill from Rhuber Lawn—
Laundry basket piles scatter along weeds.
I go through pockets, find loose change
and tea bags—mint medley and honey pomegranate.
I gather nail files and combs, a ticket from the 7-Train
to Flushing Meadows.
I'm too ashamed to stay and clean up the mess,
so after a few minutes, I leave, unnoticed.
I go home and take a bath, then eat yogurt
and watch a William Holden flick on TCM.

Beast

I want for your words to bruise me.
For your body—burning in this spitfire day
to make my lungs cry for air.

I want you to teach me how to be ugly.
To run your crooked fingers across my face
and blemish my virgin skin.

I want the corners of my mouth dry.
Your sour breath cooling my lips
and oversized arms to staple me shut.

You are an ogre,
but I do not lament
for your tribulations.

I hide from your peacefulness;
relish in your anger.

Your tongue does nothing but fill up your mouth,
so let it hang.

Meth

Today, a miracle because no one vomits.
We eat grass like dogs, hunch on all fours
chase the white dragon until the gel in the lava lamp
resembles our bodies.

The dinosaur language he chants when he's high
gives me tremors. Seismic waves crack my earth;
I cannot walk a straight line.

I swivel, grind my teeth,
lick Reynolds Wrap.

We sit on the patio, concentrate on bridged mountains:
their concrete necks, shelves that hold their rib cages.
The rock fragments, fingernails, jut from a sheet of skin.

My cheeks swell in the presence of his tongue.
I roll it around, remember how he tastes
in September, when his sinuses thicken
and the saliva in his mouth turns to syrup.

We cool down with water
that smells like last winter's snow.
We scribble letters on the breezeway floor
with crayons, try to write our names.

Migration

All the gravity in the world
couldn't keep you from getting high.
Your fingers are small bones
that balance your blunt
as you slip into a hollow world
and create a tarried illusion of reality.

You have what it takes to make me crawl
on my knees and imitate an animal.
begging for the wrong reasons,
in preparation of this storm.

I remember the first day of the month
you were in a panicked stupor
when the snow geese flew in dozens
outside of our window, gathering
in spit-licked flocks their feathers
lining the house, and you watching
their beauty as you grabbed the windowsill.

I opened the door to watch
their abrupt explosion of flight.
I felt a powerful alertness for the sun.

But there's a danger in the timing.
One second sooner
and you could have lit your last joint
the smoke bedding your eyelids
and the birds could have flown away,
or never have been there at all.

Ripe

You told me the skin on the plum
was like the skin on your heart—
thin and easy to bite through,
that the pit in the middle
was callused and hardened,
from overuse and your hands
had trouble finding a spot that wasn't bruised.
The scars became marks that showed the small
incisors of various mouths, the twin pricks and the bitten mold.
You told me that the sky was empty
and only in our way,
that the pockets of earth we uncovered
left a trail to heaven,
and if I played my cards right
I could catch a glimpse of its fruit.

After The Break-Up

When the wind died down
I knew I was home.
Quietly, I stepped through the door
letting go of the sticky afterbirth of night.

You called me twice before I fell asleep,
each message unrelated to the next.
Last night, your penis hung limply to the side,
like a panting dog's tongue.
The fan blew loudly against my sweaty folds.

"You left almonds on my floor,"
you told me over the phone,
as if you were expecting me to come back
and clean them off the carpet.

The next morning I woke early
forgot my coffee and my jacket,
drove to work two hours early,
sat in the parking lot,
listened to NPR, and cried.

Passing Whistle Signals

The aqua sound of the attic
thrums through my head.
I crouch by a pile of old wooden spoons
and run my fingers along the edges.
These were the ones my grandmother gave me.
They were from Peru, where she met her husband
on a steamboat, twenty miles
from where she would later open her restaurant
with only the recipes she knew from her own mother.

I look at the spoons, the edges stained
from sauces and cooking oils
and think how the business held her together,
the budded razor of her heart
kept beating long after her husband passed.

I remember the damaged look she used to make
when I brought up his name,
and in the last years of her life,
she kept the ring he gave her
around her neck, because it no longer
fit on her arthritic fingers.

I think it was from all the stirring and mixing.
That's when I want to break the spoon
or throw it straight across the room.
Instead, I find myself holding it
against my chest, the face near my ear.
I listen for the sound of that steamboat.

On seeing a nude boy by the side of the diner on Beacon Street

We laugh.

Beacon Street Diner

It's all about the grease.
The waitress pours pitchers of water
with yellow cubes,
filaments of dirt settle at the bottom.

More than once we've tried to slip
Oreos into the deep fryer,
pecan pies into the blender.

I've seen Pat take orders with
her eyes closed, listening
to the buzz of the stove,
folding the tablecloths,
collecting the trays.

The humdrum of life expands
the swell in her heart.
She listens to Joni Mitchell
and sweeps stale fries
into the dustpan.

Jon the cop comes in at 8:00 promptly.
The door rattles.
I look up from my crossword
ask him if he knows a five letter word
for get out, this isn't a bar.
That doesn't seem to keep him away.

He brings in his bottle of Scotch
and slips it into his coffee,
tells me stories from the day—

rescued another kid from the water tower,
caught Margie drunk driving again,
It's all the same, he says.

Like everyone in this town,
he wants some action.
He pushes in his stool
and wobbles to the door, walks home.
It's all about the grease.

Basement Knowledge

You keep your ears and arms and hands
ready to go at a moment's notice.
You are always alert,
set to defend yourself in any situation.

Your dad taught you to keep your guard up—
late nights in the basement watching
boxing matches and throwing punches.
He told you never to strike first
but only to act in self-defense.

Those are the nights you remember most,
sneaking down to the basement
after mother had gone to bed,
talking with your dad,
sipping a little of his coffee,
and sniffing the cigar
until it burned your nose.

The next morning, your mother couldn't
wake you in time for the school bus,
but you didn't mind your tardiness.
because you learned more in a night from dad
than you ever would in your
first period history class.

When I take off my shirt

His breath—the bricked-baked vanilla wind
leaves patterns across my skin.

They remind me of abstract paintings.
His forehead wrinkles like crumpled paper.

He sits on the floor picks the carpet,
bites his lip, forgets to blink.

Outside the Beacon Street traffic
crawls along, unnoticed.
My virginity is a spark plug,
I can't take my mind off the ignition.

My glass-bell sighs are placed before his great exhale.
These breasts, two over-easy eggs,

the yolks, unbroken
until his spatula hand ruins breakfast.

Children don't play *Marco Polo* around here, they play *Charlie Pyle*.

It was the quiet kid you had to look out for
on Beacon Street, one day he was writing
science fiction stories, the next
he was gone.

We wouldn't discover Charlie Pyle until three
years later, his body buried under sediment,
worms crawling through the sockets of his skull.
I think one of the Benson twins found him.

The police snatched his corpse before
you could say *investigation.*
That was the last we ever heard of him

until last Halloween when Miss Cooper
awoke at 4 a.m. and came running into
the police station screaming
that she'd seen his ghost.
I'd never seen the hair
on an old lady stand straighter.

I never told anyone, but later that next evening,
I crept into Miss Cooper's
ratty old place, took the Ouija board
my grandfather left me,
and asked Charlie how he died.
The air felt colder for a moment,
and I listened. There was a rattling
on the window, and I tried
to open it, but it slammed shut.
I ran out of her house
in a sprint, the sweat dripping cold
down the back of my neck like ice.

Beacon Street Annual Cocktail Party

The cocktail party was a hit.
I had three martinis, the olive's open eye
winking at me. You had bourbon on the rocks,
at least five glasses.

I wore long silver gloves up to my elbows,
you took your suit off the hanger,
smoothed it at the shoulders and draped
it over your hunched spine.

You were in the process of
surrendering, in your eyes I saw sailors
walking away, oars paddling toward shore.

I bit down on crumpled appetizers,
bacon scallops, flesh bitten sushi.
The other girls wore evening gowns,
I wore a rose petal.

This is how we pretend we're alright.
You come by every half hour,
brush against my earlobe, pretend to whisper something
romantic, instead you ask me:
what the fuck I'm wearing.

I smile, bite my olive, tell you to learn how
to use a fucking iron. You grab another drink.
Your sixth? Seventh? I've lost count.
I twist the stem of a cherry around my tongue
like a piece of licorice.
You've lost your flavor.

The dancing begins, insects burrowing into wood,
clicking to a beat. You are nowhere to be found.
My fat features reflect off of mirrors.
There are two dozen of me, none of you.

The boundaries of all things beautiful

When I learned to love him a second time,
I had to revisit the cracks in his body,
places where time had slowed him,
made him frail.

He told me about the time he tried
to jump off the Beacon Street Bridge
swirl like a liver in the water.
I covered my mouth when I coughed
so the copies of him wouldn't echo forward.

I rub the yellow bruises with cloth,
tell him to lean forward so I don't pinch the skin.
He tries to talk with his cotton tongue

"We should join the geese,"
he says, his alabaster skin shines
as he looks into the distance.
Days like today
I'm always afraid of what he sees.

Exodus

Then it was Christmas
and we were sewing squares on jeans
to give to the orphans.
You were in the church pew lighting a cigarette
with a smile on your face
and a copy of *Catcher In The Rye*
folded between your knees.
I told you smoking wasn't allowed in this chapel,
and you were moping the rest of the night
until Rusty came home
and brought you a dead field mouse.
You pet Rusty between the ears
where he liked it,
told him what a great dog he was,
then went out back to the lawn
and took your bow and arrow
and a sack of white powder
and walked into the cornfield.
You never came back.

III. The Land

At the Well

I am a sponge.

I have heard rumors of the water's
healing strength. I soak in it
to squeeze back at the world.

My clothes sag as I wade
through water, my rosary beads
jingle around my wrist.

The hours web into knots,
stationary hands stuck in a final position.

Time slips, and I am caught
between cracked cups of light.

My skin is a river of pulse.
It suffers.

Let's pretend the mountains are our husbands

she whispers, claims the peak with the most snow,
says it will keep her warm, a deer hide.
I pose and curtsey to the land,
skim the tops of the Appalachians—
their heavy chests piles of rock, sturdy.
The birds give me energy: I watch as they circle.
I stretch out my hands like I'm flying.
Stand tall in the open field, to prove
I am vertical.

The prime meridian rips itself in half to accommodate for my presence

I wear a stethoscope to hear nature's respirations.
It pours out by the river, a metronome.

Afraid of the land
I walk so quickly.
I do not stop
to watch the possum.

My eyes are red from the sun
or the pollen (it takes up the air).

I examine a moon rock
its crevices and curves.
Every once in a while
we need a day to consult with nature,
walk through the woods, and forget.

On the hottest day of the year

I woke up in the trash.
The night before,
we drank cold cans of Corona
until our mouths tasted like sweat.
We never learned about cleanliness
on Beacon Street.
The garbage collectors
played poker in the pick-up trucks
while the waitresses sucked
on cigars and swept bits of food
from the tablecloths with their hands.
We strolled through the landfill
as the sky bruised purple
picking and feeding and fending
off our neighbors who tried
to steal our trash, dumpster divers.
We found coins and paperclips,
old bottle caps and clothes.
I stripped down to my skin
wading through the junkyard
dirty as a skunk,
carrying an armful of treasures.

Stirrings

At night the lawn gnomes go missing.
We can hear them walk
along the border of the dried up fish pond in our yard.

Beacon Street Lake, 8:55 p.m.

The high pitched moon signals
me forward, lowers its light.

I shiver in the darkness, as I tiptoe
across the lake, *just being here.*

I watch the snakes slide
into mud. The golden moss lungs
of the earth tangle around my legs.

The bugs gather like halos,
hover over my head.

I enter the mouth of a small cave,
the sides drip like glue melting in the heat of the day.

I'm not afraid. I catch a spider,
her black fur tickles my fingers.
I gently peel back each of her eight legs.
There are ways to admit your
crumbling.

Garden Soliloquy

The way your life was planted
is a reminder of the ground
I break. Every afternoon as I dig in the garden,
the black crows circle overhead,
and I am reminded of you chasing them
frantically out by the barn,
a sweat mustache over your upper lip
and pit stains under your arms.
You were a fighter.
Thirteen rounds of chemotherapy
and the entire New Testament,
and you swore you would be well again.
I thought so too,
when I made you fresh eggs from the farm
over whole wheat toast and you told me
you were going to spend a week
at the cabin, hiking the trails
and fishing by the moonlight.
The next morning,
I took you to the hospital
with swollen lips and leaky eyes
and you slipped under the sheets.
The stalks in the field by your window
growing tall, your own roots withering.
If only I could help you,
let you have some of its soil.

Fever 102

I am born from innocence.
A drip
      from violated sky.

The cauldron of night leaks into day.
With strips of my body gone
small seconds left in the universe.

This Frayed Universe

The day rises in installments;
I open my eyes to the fused film of fog.

I wake in the absence of disaster
and fill my cup with bruises.

I'm allergic to air
I tell him, my hair is a mess. I rake and unravel knots.

I peel like a sunburn,
a small speck in this frayed universe.

My knees are rug-burned and bare,
they slide against the carpet in my collapse.

I want to be his pollen in the mornings
a patchwork piece of poetry,

but I'm a torn cloth, a crater
in the center of his earth.

I stand, let the faucet rinse my chapped hands
the sun squeezes like lotion through the window.

Its rays dress me, and he watches
as the light dances along my hips.

Here, in The Realm of Everything

I have come to rely on the air to fill
the crevices in my body.

Heavy, I drop at my father's feet.
He half-holds me like a bag of apples,

I drip winesap, gala.
He examines me, finds my rough spots
brown holes where worms chewed through,
left me softened.

We sit up all night
stir our thoughts into tea
until the sun squeezes up over the hill.

I'm reminded of the stove's open eye
when dad lit a cigarette from the burner
because I hid all the lighters.

I want him to know this:
If I could find a way to escape
this whale-belly world, I would.

Red-Handed

When the Donaldson's house burned down,
we each took a piece of rubble as a souvenir.

I remember walking by the bushes on the way to school
and thinking how edible the redcurrants looked.

I wanted to taste the bulbs, but my brother slapped my hand away,
told me if I ate them I would die. I was always tempted.

After the fire I held my piece of tarnished rubble
wanting so badly to see if the bushes were still alive.

I walked down the path while nobody was looking
and made it to the redcurrant clearing.

They were hanging—a massacre of thorns
and a forecast of red, but I was exuberant.

I ran to the first bush and plucked
a berry from its grip.

I held the surface to my nose, took
in the scent of almost-death and rubbed it across my lips.

A soft film of residue spread along the outline,
and I even took the edge to my teeth,

gently biting and breaking the surface.
A tart taste filled me, and I took pleasure in its bitterness.

"What are you doing?" a small voice made me jump,
and I instantly spit out the berry,

its withered casing, caught
on a branch. I turned and ran away from the house,

Mrs. Donaldson calling after me
that the berries tasted great in pies.

Winter Shrine

Your deep crystal face is cut
out of the January landscape.
You are the backdrop of winter.
I peer out the window, the trees
line the yard's frame like grizzled gnomes
with great beards,
they are whispers of white
among the fallen snow,
or the swan neck of the great planes
as the mountains huddle over
our bodies, our protection.

Seasonal Affective Disorder

Winter is falling into knots around my wrists.
I'll restore the roots
when my body breaks this sadness.

Love Poem, 4:00

In the oval of this hour
I find myself in a tunnel of throat
clinging to your body like Saran wrap.

You turn me into a mind of forget.
I have to call back to life the objects
that used to be—

the porcelain kettle on the stove
that frightens Mr. Paws,
the fine china my mother found
at the flea market, while I was busy
rampaging the record man for
a vintage Jerry Lee Lewis
for a nickel and some pocket lint
because I thought "The Killer's" jawline
was sexy.

You carry me to the beach
with your strong arms,
a sway about your body.
This is the first tropical storm
of the summer
and the steady rain tastes like salt.

The remainder of the day
won't fill this way.
I'll have to occupy my thoughts
to make up for the sense
of longing I will have
for your soft breath against my face
the steadiness of your arms
and the way you lay me
on the sand
so I feel as if I'm floating.

Kingdom Come

We walk the yellow lands in search of power
scour its depths like a dragon's tongue.

We know there is no shield big enough
to cover the area of our skin.

I kick through salt mines of rocks
hoping to touch the tips of crowns

wash my body away from the sand,
change this stone on my finger into a diamond.

We can't say why we are predictable.
Only humans as hands as hardened hearts.

Replanting the Garden

I'm held accountable for the earth's language.
I dig a hole and place geraniums in pockets,
soft pink lips covered in dirt.

Tired of the wind, how it picks up seeds,
scatters them in valleys. I massage the ground,
feel for artifacts, scars of roots
or shrubs that can be re-grown.

In every breeze I'm the destroyer.
I step on plant crusts, crush colonies of ants,
pluck daffodils off unsteady stems.

I know each of the stretches of land
like they're my own children,
name them and watch them grow.

I hold out my hand for plump bees to gather,
for the praying mantis to pray for me.
I listen as the marble voices of the treetops
rustle leaves, whispering my purpose.

Polluted with age and all used up,
I head for the ocean.
Leave behind this beautiful life,
my buckshot oblivion.

On Beacon Street, Part III

Children still are born cross-eyed with gall.
They still gather like minnows in a small scale pond.
They still throw acorns at neighborhood houses,
They still root through the dumpster at 2:00 in the morning.

Old Man Tucker died at home with his Rottweiler.
His funeral was on a Tuesday,
There's always a wave of apologies before a memorial.
When the long light reaches the casket,
we are reminded of a statue, or a Gargoyle.

Arrow Landing is crawling with snakes,
the swamp is perfect in the summer months.
The heat closes in on our bodies
and we drip-sweat our sins.

The congregation settles,
the traffic patterns flow
out from the center like veins.
I pick up a rock
pitch it over my shoulder
toward the sky.
The ascent is a glorious one.

Sarah Brashear lives in Annville, PA and teaches
writing at Lebanon Valley College and Harrisburg Area
Community College. She is also the Assistant Tennis
Coach at Lebanon Valley College. She has an MFA in
Creative Writing from Chatham University.

49008106R00049

Made in the USA
Charleston, SC
17 November 2015